The Listening Attention

Bob Fergeson

TAT Foundation Press

Published by TAT Foundation Press
47 Washington Avenue #150
Wheeling, West Virginia 26003
www.tatfoundation.org

All photos copyright © 2009 Robert Fergeson
Cover Photo: Sunrise, LaSal Mountains, Utah
Back Cover: Moon Set, Bayou Cane, Louisiana
www.nostalgiawest.com

Text font: Palatino Linotype

Main entry under title: *The Listening Attention*

1. Spirituality   2 Philosophy

Library of Congress control number:
2010931176

ISBN: 978-0-9799630-6-3

The Listening Attention

Gateway to Within

In the spiritual search, the quest for true self-definition, we soon come to the realization that our best efforts, and even our very selves, are mechanical and reactive. No matter how subtle or astute our meditation may be, we will never realize nirvana by using yet another facet of samsara. A different level of seeing is needed, a pure awareness that is not itself a product of the world or mind, but primary to the reaction pattern we call ourselves. A looking which is attentive, yet not reactive. A listening which is not affected by circumstance and the constant changes of the mind. Such an attention would lie outside of time and space, beyond circumstance, yet be aware of them as well as itself. Such a Listening Attention would also be directly connected to the formless inner realm of our True Self, and provide a Gateway to Within.

Contents

Gateway to Within

I see only what you see, but I notice what I see.
— Ramana Maharshi

I only see what you see, but I have trained myself,
Doctor Watson, to notice what I see.
— Sherlock Holmes

The above quotations point to something valuable, to what we might call a second attention. There are three parties involved, rather than the usual two. There is the looker, or the person, and what is seen: the world, or outer environment. Together they make up our reactive pattern, the duality of the mind. The one referred to who "notices" is something different. This noticing, or second Looker, sees the entire game, or mind realm, but is not affected by it. It has no active interest in the game, being passive, but notices the game entire. It is active only in its attention, not in its reaction. This Listening Attention sees both ways at once; outwardly towards the mind, and inwardly towards the Unknown. It forms a bridge, or gate, between the outer and Inner man. The angst that many feel, the undefined suffering of the average man, is due to this loss of connection with his Inner Self.

How can we re-connect, open the Gateway to Within, and once more gain the Peace and Understanding of our Inner Self? First, we may need to remove any obstacles and mis-conceptions that block us and keep us from being able to listen to the voice within. Many Tricks and Traps can stop us, and we may doubt if it's a worthwhile endeavor, this stalking our-selves. We must connect with those who have been within and can point the way, and establish links to our fellow seekers and their experience.

The Place of No Concern

In the winter of 2000, something happened to me that answered my questions as to who I am and my relationship to life and death, the questions that had somehow haunted me, consciously or not, for most of my adult life. Soon after this event, I wrote in my notes, "I was taken beyond myself into the place of no concern." The years of wandering, of alternating between pleasure and misery, came to an end, along with the searching and longing it generated. Paradoxically, I saw that in all that time I had never really moved. Rather, I simply woke up.

At the time of this occurrence, I was participating in an online confrontation group, my interest in spiritual matters being at a peak. A period of despair had thankfully passed, in which I had mostly given up hope of ever finding anything more than a little peace of mind, and perhaps something to do to pass the years. The online group helped provide the tension needed to push my spiritual interest back to the forefront.

I had been getting glimpses of how the mind works in dividing the personality into opposites, such as the parent/child, ego1/ego2, and God/Charlie Brown, and was determined to somehow transcend this trap. One of the members of the group artfully confronted me, suggesting that something I should look at was how I was in love with my self, the very thing I was trying to separate from. Realizing I was being fooled again, trapped in yet another duality, I came to a dead end. I can't remember the details of the exchange, but it dropped like a depth charge into my mind. Acting as a catalyst, it soon caused a change. This change was something I could not have foreseen, for it was a total change in being, rather than in thought.

I remember sitting on my bed, looking toward the mirror in the bathroom, and suddenly noticing I was no longer the same. It's still very difficult to explain this. It was not a change in thought or feeling, but rather a change in place or perspective. I was no longer "in the world," but back beyond some inner boundary separating the formal from the informal. It was not traumatic, but rather curious. One of the first things I noticed was that I could see "Bob," but he could not see me. I thought this strange, and wrote in my notes that he seemed to be asleep or hypnotized, so involved in the world that he could not look back. I soon discovered that he was entirely of the world, being solely the product of experience, and thus incapable of seeing anything else. The poem on page 15, "The Little Man," came to me at the time in an attempt to describe this first event.

This state continued unabated for a couple of weeks. I spent the time watching Bob, the Little Man, as he went about his day-to-day business, marveling at my newfound lack of concern or worry, though Bob clung to his with his usual fervor. There was no change in the field of emotion coming directly from this change, or answers to any questions, only an interest in how strange it was to find myself completely unattached to thought, emotion, the world, and anything else one might call existence, even though it was all there for the seeing. My attention had been freed from its fixation on and in the personality, though its direction was still outward turned only. This too, was about to change.

One day off a couple of weeks later, I was out cross-country skiing. I was climbing a long ridge. The slow, easy ascent would take a couple of hours, freeing my thoughts to go where they may. I was relaxed, being in familiar territory where I felt safe, free from worry or concern. As I continued up the hill, I felt that something was trying to get my attention, that perhaps there was someone behind me. I turned around, but was alone on the hill. Still, I could not shake the feeling. It grew steadily though quietly. I soon came to see that it was not in the surroundings, but somewhere within the inner field of the mind. It was as if a still voice were saying, "turn round and look within, and all you seek will be answered." So, I did. As I looked within at whatever this silent prodding was, a dam burst, and my long pent up questioning could no longer be contained. Over the next couple of hours, all my questions were answered, as my attention was now free to go into the mysterious unknown source within, from which all springs.

I saw, without a shadow of a doubt, that whatever looked out from my eyes, was the same in all men. There was no individual, but only Universal Man. Now this was traumatic. It ran counter to the dualistic belief I held that I was either better than, or worse than, everyone else. Not only was I the same, I didn't even exist! As the stream of false notions I took as my "self" came to the surface, they were burned away in the light of truth that was so obviously present, but had been hidden within. I became more and more shaken, and soon found myself lying in the snow, weeping. I came to see that everything was in the same place, at the same time. That everything is One, contained in Nothing. All was possible, all was available, depending on what the Heart desired, and the Heart desired nothing but Itself. Nothing was separate, for no things existed.

At this point, something inside me stopped the process. At the time I thought that "something" saw that something was about to break, and this must not happen. The journey within was halted. I slowly came back to the senses and noticed I was becoming a bit numb from lying in the snow. I shook myself off, got back on my skis and began the long descent to the highway and town. On the way more energy knots, as I've come to call them, were unloosed, as long held beliefs were seen through and discarded. By the time I got home, I was able to reflect on what had happened. I now knew what I was, though I still cannot describe it very well. This "seeing" is still available, though the "oneness with the One" has receded to a faint thread or feel. I can't see how one could function if it were otherwise. Whenever I return to that place in the woods, something of the feeling of what happened still returns.

In the coming weeks, the two incidents began to make sense. The first, the separation of the attention from its fixation in the personality, was the *becoming*. I had heard this term for years, but always interpreted it as becoming something manifest, some "thing" in the world of thought or mind, such as smarter, bigger, more subtle, wiser; the Big Man. Never would I have seen it for the complete change it was. Never would I have seen that to become, I had first to unbecome, to recede into non-existence. I remember thinking at the time that whatever I had become, it was something unhuman, meaning that I could no longer find *any attributes* in what I now was, other than what might be called awareness.

The second event was the *dissolving* of the emotional attachments, or energy knots, which held the attention tightly bound to the unreal assumptions I had taken as reality. I saw that I had taken my very meaning, and placed my highest value, on inherited beliefs, from top to bottom. Now, nothing was my own, for there was no longer anyone to claim anything. Thus, I had freedom to simply see and listen. I no longer had to place my very sense of being in the world of thought and mind. I Was, and that was All. Paradoxically, "Bob" is still pretty much the same. Perhaps a bit more relaxed, but still in and of the world, a reaction pattern without any real existence of his own.

In hindsight, I cannot say I know how all this happened in detail, except to say that I had a bit of luck, a few good friends, and could not rest until I knew what I was and had some real understanding of what was going on in terms of life and death. I had a mantra that expressed the inner angst I felt at not being defined: "I don't know what's going on, but I'm going to find out." I also cannot express the gratitude I feel to several persons who were part of this. Nothing in the search is more valuable than those whose honest concern for your long-term peace takes precedence over the pettiness of your ego. As the years go by, I still find that my home is in the Place of No Concern, as is yours. Will you use the life you have as a return ticket?

The Little Man

From early morning coffee
to late night herbal tea,
We lived for near forever,
the Little Man and me.

When first I came to travel
in this classroom wide and grand,
I knew nothing of the coming
of this lonely Little Man.

But parents, teachers, doctors,
the whole damn Helping Herd,
Soon created him inside me,
As their ancestors had insured.
He has no real existence,
None that I can see.
But could and should and would!
Screamed the Little Man in me.

Soon I hid myself in pride,
Found that fear blocked every door.
I was now what I despised!
Just as those that'd gone before.

The hypnosis worked its magic,
No peace had I, no stand.
Just a mis-identification,
I became the Little Man.
I took him for a person,
Hell, I thought that he was me!
He sure could be convincing,
that Little Man in me.

Then one day it happened,
I know not really why,
I looked out there below me
From some Great Eternal Sky.
He didn't even notice,
So busy as a bee,
He just kept right on sleeping, but
that Little Man ain't me!

One day looking in the mirror,
From my bed as I did stand,
I receded back behind him,
that sleeping Little Man.
He didn't even notice,
Just a grain lost in the sand,
He can't look back and see me,
that lonely Little Man.

I watch him and his pattern,
How he blends right in so well,
That his life and his surroundings
are no different from himself.
He has no greater vision,
Desire and fear are all he sees.
An actor in the TV,
that Little Man in me.

It's a sad but true short story,
I cry a tear, and so does he,
He won't survive, he lives to die,
the Little Man in me.

A Worthwhile Endeavor

This is about what I call the "Listening Attention," a meditation technique, if you will, which I've found to be a gateway to our Inner Self. The poet John Davis once said he felt the highest meditation was "listening with the eyes." This is a good starting definition. Another would be to look with attention, but without interpretation: to listen, the attention turned both inward and outward at the same time, with no thought or expectation. No expectation, judging or defining; no thought, no mind. This combined attention uses both the inner ear and eye, and is turned towards the inner heart and the outer world simultaneously. It is passive in that it does not project an image, or thought; it is active for the same reason, in that it is a pure attention, an active not-doing. There is no sense of an "I" involved, for that would mean the springing forth of an image, which the attention would become identified with. It does not entail a motionless, inert body, for it can be found while engaging in activity.

Before talking about how to find this portal to the Inner Self, let's first explore why it would be a worthwhile endeavor. First, I'd like to clarify that this is not a technique for adding another "spiritual" behavior to our list. We do not need to put another head on top of the one we already have, but need to somehow get back to a truer state we have lost through years of conditioning. In other words, we do not need another form of hypnosis or new way to put ourselves further to sleep, but to find how to become un-hypnotized, more awake. I have to assume if you've come this far that you have reasons for engaging in spiritual work. Enough time spent digging through the patterns and habits of the mind will eventually lead one to the unflattering realization that one is mechanical, a robot. I like to call this creature we find ourselves to be, a SMAARP, a Self-Maintaining Accidental Associative Reaction Pattern. Most of us start this journey to self-discovery convinced we are smart SMAARP's, and it can take quite a few blows to our proverbial fat heads before we realize we are mechanical, that the mind can never solve the problem of self-definition by itself. We need help. The listening attention is a door to going within, to re-connecting with our inner man, to that part of us which Knows. Once we are convinced of our robotic nature, we may come to see the value of connecting once again with the intelligence that created us.

The silent passage to the inner world is always with us, it does not need to be formed, just found, but we may need years of preparation to see it. A great deal of self-analysis, "work on one-self," is usually needed in order to get beyond the ego and its belief that the mind and worded thoughts will lead us to the Real. A lifetime of learned behaviors, emotional blocks, fears, self-doubts, and wishful thinking need to be cleared away. We must reach a point where we can slip behind our compensatory thinking patterns long enough to let something real get through. All repressed emotional material and debilitating drains on our energy must be dealt with, too. We will need all our strength to face the unknown, alone and unarmed.

There will be much resistance to the attempt to go within. Our physical needs must be met, giving us the thought that time spent "doing nothing but listening" is sheer folly. The need for distraction in social endeavors, TV, movies, and other forms of feeding the head, will need to be dealt with. Our family and friends will most likely not share the value we place on finding a connection to the Inner Self, as it does not bring an immediate material reward and is not conducive to maintaining whatever psychological dramas might be in place.

Perhaps the most effective resistance to our inner journey will not come from outside, through society or family, but from our own fear of the unknown. We may find we are both unwilling to let go of our old way of being, and not willing to take a chance on something new. For most of us, some form of suffering or trauma is necessary before we will trust our own inner guidance. Fear can block us at every turn, until we take our meaning from within, from the present, and release our mental hold on the projected past or imagined future.

These struggles of self-discovery are also necessary to find the right individual method for the listening attention. I found that moving about, through hiking and cross country skiing, to be the best way for me. I could not sit still long enough to bring about the inner relaxation needed, or else would simply fall asleep. I know of one man who would drive, spending hours behind the wheel of his car because it would give his outer mind and body just enough to do to allow his inner self the freedom to surface. If sitting in a chair will work, great, it would sure save a lot of time and gas. Knowing what body type and disposition we have is a great help in opening the door.

A good example of how this can happen was during one winter as I was struggling to improve my cross-country skiing technique. I was caught between the technical advice given by instructor friends, and the feeling that I knew what to do if I would just listen to the inner voice instead. I finally decided to go with my instincts, and my skiing quickly reached a new level of freedom and skill. Affirmation was quick in coming, for one day as I was thumbing through a skiing magazine, I noticed an article by a coach on what techniques the fastest skiers used. The system he described was exactly the one I had found, and had been discovered by his athletes in much the same way. While this may hardly seem a momentous step in self-discovery, it gave the clue that trusting my own intuition and inner guidance was a good idea, and that rote learning through mimicking others would not bring me any closer to learning to go within. Everyone must find his own portal into the listening attention through his own experience and faith.

Stalking Yourself with the Listening Attention

Above the door to the ancient temple in Delphi were inscribed the words, "Know Thyself." These words describe the process by which we separate from our false state of ignorance and rediscover true Being. But how do we initiate this process, this grand work of spiritual discovery? What tools should we choose to come to know this thing we call "ourselves"? If we are to engage in the pursuit of self-definition we will need to use the best tools available. To stalk our "self," we will need something above or behind this personality to best observe with, something of a different order. Using the personality to observe the personality simply doesn't work. It's like trying to lift a plank while standing on it. This self we wish to come to know is a constantly changing, moving target, a veritable chain of reactions and patterns, seldom still, but always within our sight. To observe it we will need something calm and constant. Something that looks but doesn't react; a seeing that listens.

Spending time alone, in a quiet environment, can be a good way to start this practice of self-observation. To be free of the routines of work and family and the expectations of society is calming and conducive to beginning the art of introspection. We can let our guard down a bit. Also, our own personality is partially absent.

The part of us that interfaces with others is no longer needed and we can relax. This state of lack of attack can be quite useful for sneaking a look at ourselves. Since other people do not have to be dealt with, we can devote all of our energy to watching the only person that remains: our self. The social personality is a tool whose job is to deal with social survival. It has been made to do this, in and by the social context, and is only answerable to that context. To try to use it for examining the self, as we normally use it to examine others, will not work. It may not be the best tool we have to better know ourselves. A hammer is only a fitting tool when combined with nails and wood. To observe the files in our computer, we need something with a subtler touch. A listening attention is needed, a looking without speaking, an interior silence that observes but does not place value.

Eckhart Tolle gives a good example of the type of attention we need. He asks us to try a little experiment, to close your eyes and say to yourself, "What's my next thought going to be?" then become very alert and wait for this next thought, just as if you were a cat silently watching a mouse hole. What thought is going to pop out? As long as we are in this alert silent watching/listening, no associative thought pattern interferes with our observing. Let's take the experiment a bit further and put ourselves in the context of the hunter or stalker. Our goal is to stalk ourselves. The personality and ego are our game. We wish to observe them, not observe through them. Our game is very smart for it knows what we are thinking, even before we think it, for it has had control over us for years, perhaps decades. The only advantage we have is our simple, pure awareness, something the ego lacks. We must become very still and alert, as if we were in a room with a large beast, which can only grab us if we move, feel, or even think. As long as we observe without placing meaning on our observation, we are invisible, and can watch the beast, freely and calmly. If ever the thought comes to us, "Hey, I'm watching myself" or, "Wow, look what I'm doing," we have lost the thread. We are then reacting, not observing. Watch for this "I" thought. If the feeling of "I" and its sense of being the "doer" come into the scene, the listening attention is lost, and you're off the track.

At first we will only be able to watch ourselves during quiet times, such as meditation. While our quarry is relatively still, we are not confused by its movements and are able to hold our attention steady. Later, we can observe when the personality is more active, and can keep from being thrown off balance. It's good to learn to swim in shallow quiet waters, before taking on the waves. Once the basic feel of the listening attention is found, one can progress from observing oneself in quiet times to watching the body and mind as they perform small repetitive tasks. Eventually the awareness will become free enough to observe the self, or "person," in complex actions such as conversation. As we begin to see more and more of ourselves, we gain a certain freedom. Its value does not lie in the modifying of our behavior into a more efficient, flattering form, but simply in becoming free from the hypnotic identification with our pattern. We begin to see we truly do not do and never have. We only observe.

No matter how determined we are to stalk this strange person we call ourselves, we will continue to fall asleep and be swept back into the state of identification. One tool we can make use of to counter this is what might be called "alarm clocks." We create little habits that remind us of our task: which is to watch silently. We place these alarms throughout our day. An example is meditating at a fixed time. The body will become used to this and remind us it's time to turn inward and observe. Another is books or tapes we find to have value. These can serve as alarms by their presence, as well as by their content. One of the best is a group of fellow seekers, who can serve as mirrors of our current state and help snap us back on track. As with anything done with regular routine, these alarms will become less useful with habit, and new ones will be needed.

Another trick is to practice what is called "inner stop." Whenever we sense we are becoming obsessed with a thought pattern, fantasy or habit, whether of anger, self-pity or desire, we can say to ourselves, "Stop!" Just as a loud unexpected noise can stop the conversation in a room, so can this command silence the noise in our head.

One last pointer is what might be called developing 360-degree vision. This is best described as having a two-pronged awareness. One arrow is pointed outwards, towards the relative world and the "person." The other is aimed inward, towards our source. Our quarry, or what we might call the person, can only look out. We have a distinct advantage in being directly connected to that Infinite Silence within and its unlimited patience and wisdom.

Coming to know ourselves eventually crushes the ego, in that we find we are not what we imagined ourselves to be. We begin to see that the person we think we are is purely mechanical, a robot. Honesty and courage will be needed if we are to accept what we see, and perseverance when we find our task difficult and wish to retreat back into imagination. This process of dis-identifying leads to ego-death, as we separate from our pattern. The simple act of clearly seeing the person we were for what it truly is, is enough to bring about its death. We find we have become that which witnesses experience, where before we were experience, creating more and more experiences in an endless mechanical pattern. We are no longer the wily animal we have been tracking, which becomes cleverer with every experience, but instead something free, eternal, and indescribable.

Cautionary Notes

1. There is an easy trap to fall into when we first engage in self-observation, and that is to create, or visualize, an observer who observes. We are then back in the same comfortable game we were in in the first place: that of the personality reacting to the environment in an endless pattern. There is no sentience in mechanical reaction. In describing observation, we are not talking about visualization or imagination, but the simple act of looking without reaction, of looking through the personality, not with it. We have been taught since birth to create and then identify with a separate thing we call ourselves. This reaction pattern continually recreates itself as the person who reacts.

2. Right Intent. We can only use the listening attention for gaining self-knowledge, knowledge of our own mind. If ambition, ego, or greed comes into play, we have degraded into visualization and are lost. We must want only to scrutinize the self and observe the mind. We must not, and will not be allowed to, take advantage of or gloat over our success. We can take the example of Joseph Sadony to heart. After using his psychic gifts to provide a friend with profitable information in the financial market, he lost his powers for one year to the day. He never again traded his Connection for profit.

3. We must have a stable and clear emotional state to succeed. Emotional problems cannot be of a level that spins us out of control. The capacity to walk a straight line, without being

sidetracked or continually distracted, is impera-
tive. If we attempt to go into inner silence only
to find we are full of unconscious emotional
turmoil, then these problems must be dealt with
first. To take responsibility for ourselves and to
support ourselves, to harbor no excuses; this
is the good householder, the level from which
we begin. No victims or perpetrators are found
in the journey through the valley of death. We
must first become a healthy moral animal before
we become the hunter, or the beast will hunt us.

Intelligent Spontaneity

Any wine will get you high.
Judge like a king, and choose the purest,
the ones unadulterated with fear, of some urgency about
"what's needed."
Drink the wine that moves you
as a camel moves when it's untied,
and is just ambling about. — Rumi

I've spoken before about how the listening attention is the gateway to within. This can be also spoken of as the link between the real and unreal, the manifest and unmanifest. The Christian mystics refer to the Son who is the link to the Father. William Samuel speaks of the Child as the pathfinder, and tells us it is essential to actually get in touch with this Child of Light. These refer to an essential part of us, a part that is free from the world, yet sees the world, and can lead us back to our Home in the Father. What is this Child, this intuitive light, this innocence somehow imbibed with wisdom?

One thing it is not, is childishness. It is not needy and wanting its own way, nor dependent on the things of this world for its satisfaction or existence. In fact, the Child is much better described by what it is not than what it is. Jesus once remarked that we should become as innocent as doves but also as wise as serpents. We do not use the Child for the further purposes of the ego, but become it. The listening attention is not the problem solving or even the categorizing mind, but that which simply sees or listens, and can link to a higher intelligence. Many of our problems are better solved by asking for an answer from within, then practicing patience until the answer appears. The saying, "I'll sleep on it" refers to this in a simple way; we ask, then wait until we receive.

Maurice Nicoll speaks of the puer eternus, Latin for eternal boy or child. He calls this the intermediary, the one who connects us with the higher centers within. He refers to our organism as composed of different "centers" or minds, each having its own purpose. These centers are divided into higher and lower, the lower being what we are ordinarily aware of as mind. The higher centers are said to be constantly trying to reach us, but cannot get through due to the wrong working of the lower ones. This is likened to static, negative unnatural patterns taking up most of the energy of these centers, so that they can no longer hear the higher ones; there is too much interference. Nicoll tells us that *The object of the Work is to cleanse our lower centers, to clear them out, to open their windows, so that they can begin to transmit these ideas and directions coming from higher centers.* We cannot hear the Child, who hears the Father, for the mind has become lost in the static of the world, outward turned and saturated with useless worry and dreams, broadcasting its static miasma so nothing else can get through.

This brings us to the first step to the listening attention: the clearing out of this static. Much like a radio that must be tuned in order to pick up the desired station, we must tune our machine, our lower centers, in order to pick up the constant but unheard signal of our higher self. As Rumi says, we have become obsessed with "what's needed" and have thus lost our innocence. We can no longer sit in silence and listen to what may be speaking to us: a still small voice from within.

Samuel also speaks of the value of trauma or suffering in weeding out the ego's insistence that it is the only source. For most of us, it takes a shock to turn us within. To become aware that there is something higher than ourselves permits the Child to come forth, for we begin to listen in another direction, with other ears. We come to see that there is another source of wisdom other than that of memory or the brain. We learn what intuition is, and how it works.

This clearing out of the "old man" gives room for the new, the Child. A new kind of intelligence becomes possible, one that is spontaneous, yet wise. We use our attention to not only view the world and its problems, but to also turn back within and connect with our innate intelligence. This double-pointed arrow of attention lends a certain realness. We are no longer lost in the world, for now we have become superior to it, not just in word, but in fact. The ego is seen for what it is through the eyes of the Child, and is no longer our identity or sole reference. Peace blossoms from within. The Child is born, and the Father now sees His world through the Child.

Ghost in a Box

In the realm of spiritual seekers, many and varied are the conceptions of what the Final Realization will be. Most of these are meaningless discussions of symptoms, rather than any serious attempt at understanding the final state, much less becoming It. The projected outcomes of these students are as varied as the different schools and teachers in which they place their trust. Given this Gordian Knot of thinking and feeling, fueled by ego, and projected by unexamined minds, what can one do, and expect? How can a serious seeker find assurance that they are on the right course, and how can one be sure that they themselves, or someone they know and trust, has had the Final Realization, a Total Answer?

First off, the final judge must be the person themselves. In order to pass beyond the duality of the finite mind, we must be aware of the trap of putting yet one more level above us. This is a never-ending game of the mind. There will always be someone out there who claims to have a higher, more complete, more total realization than what we, or our teacher, may have found. Only in our Selves can we rest. The trap of endlessly judging levels of attainment may be a way to keep our own spiritual ego afloat, but is a dangerous distraction if taken as the quest itself. We must press on within, and leave the fate of others to themselves.

The above said, there still remains the problem of the mind's ability to fool itself with its own projections. Driven by ambition, mental laziness, and fear of the Unknown, we may unconsciously decide to claim realization by virtue of these desires and fears, and take an easy out. How can we check and compare our own level of spiritual attainment and not be misled, by our mind or the minds of others? Let us take a look at the stages of spiritual becoming, and hope that the words herein will serve as a guide to keep our vector moving and on track.

There are three states or levels of being that we find in this search, before reaching what might be called the final or absolute state. The first may be called the level of experience. The second, the level of union. The third, the level of becoming.

The first level, that of experience, may be likened to someone in his room watching a television, and being identified with the characters in the dramas as they unfold on the screen. Losing contact with himself, he has become hypnotized into believing he is a character in the TV. The freedom he began with, that he was (and still Is), the innocent observer, has been lost, traded for the mind-motion of thought and feeling projected into the plastic box in front of him. He places his highest value on the screen-character with the most motion and energy, in relation to his upbringing and education by other screen characters. The more the characters move and are dominant (whether positive or negative does not matter), the more energy is expended, and the bigger the reaction that is drawn from the person. His innocence and detachment have been replaced with the sense of motion and thought, and the thrill of losing energy. Now that he is inseparable from his role in the drama, he places a high meaning on the feeling of belonging, which he now values as part of his very definition. He has fallen deep into sleep, and is dreaming the life he thinks he lives, a mere ghost in a box of motion, emotion and thought. He will evaluate a mystical experience in much the same way. If the experience has much motion, much release of energy, and if the character involved succeeds in his tasks, whether positive or negative, he will place a higher value on him, and claim his identity for his own.

This level is very basic and body oriented, having to do with visions of power and ego, and control over the environment. Any mystical experience or contact with spiritual systems or teachers a person on this level has, will be interpreted from this level. It constitutes no real change, or becoming, in what might be called the basic animal man, who, perhaps frustrated in his ambitions in normal life and society, has chosen a path of lesser resistance through fantasy for the fulfillment of his animal urge to power and dominance. He is the level of the mind and its motion, with which he is wholly identified. Fear and desire drive his every move, and he is firmly engrossed in his dreams.

The second level is only found through the disastrous failure of the first, combined with a serious inner commitment the seeker must have previously made to finding the truth about himself, at any cost. Given this commitment, he will sooner or later be rudely shaken awake from his dreams of fantasy, and forced to face the facts about himself. For a true change to occur, a true failure of the first level's ego must be brought about. His sense of personal identity, which is rooted in the fictional characters in the box, one after another, must be cut away. The resulting trauma will be in proportion to the size of the ego that was created. The symptoms of this collapse, meaning emotional and mental trauma, are individual, and should not be taken as the change itself. The possibility of the inner witness coming closer to the surface is the only important matter. The man then becomes identified with not just the individual character(s) on the screen of the TV as it continues to hold him entranced, but now becomes identified with everything that enters the universe-box from the projecting Light. His sense of self expands to include all the characters in the drama, as he gains a sense of unity with all the many dots in their coordinated dance across the screen. He may feel exalted and full of love for this picture show, and imagine this union to be the end-all of possibility. His very sense of exaltation, of still clinging to a higher and lower, with his remaining sense of being a "being," give him away.

This experience, though of a greater level than that of the first man, is still relative. He still believes himself to be a thing apart, in contact with another, though higher, Thing apart. The very idea of existence, of himself and anything else, is still intact, and unquestioned. His new profound experience is just that, and fades into a memory, though the conviction may remain. He soon finds himself back in the position of the first man, in motion and identified, subject to the environment for his feeling and concept of himself in the moment. Only in his memory and understanding is there a change. His perspective is still that of a man, a human entity, alive and living in a now conscious Cosmos, with which he is united.

For the man of union to Become, he must again suffer a complete disaster, and have an impossible bit of good luck, to boot. Through somehow seeing the still remaining dual nature of his mind, he may find the hint within that there is something of the intuition that led him this far, still in contact with him. He may see from time to time that he senses he is somehow behind himself, apart and unconcerned with the "thing" that he previously called "I." He may even experience moments of "headlessness," in which he looses his usual sense of "self" and instead sees the world without the noisy filter of his mind. He may even have the intuition that the secret to Becoming lies in this detachment, and not in the blissful union he values so much. This detachment has yet to become a steady factor in the present moment, but he begins to sense that the unaffected yet somehow aware screen, the very capacity for existence, and not the mind-made images that run across it in an ever-changing flux, is his true nature. That the Light and the screen it illuminates are but two different aspects of the same thing: Himself. Intuition now plays the bigger part, with reason and logic now only functions of the practical aspect of his environment.

Many little hints may come to him now, and if he is lucky enough to place a value on them, and follow them, he will continue to move. Most of these hints are along the lines of what has been called "headlessness," or the "listening attention." He may find he is observing without labeling or judging. That he is now free, for a moment, to gaze upon the world without knowing what he sees. These moments may be accompanied by a strange feeling of peace or silence, which he may come to know as the quiescence of his mind. Here, the former work on fear and desire come to fruit, as one cannot look into the Unknown if any vestige of fear or worldly ambition are still dominant. The site of the world without the minds' interpretation can be frightening for those still attached to its false security. By continuing to look within, he may sense that the Light he feels, is not only healing him, but has a direction, a Source. If he travels back far enough to merge with this Source, he may find It to be the opposite of the "world," and hence come to the possibility of triangulating the difference between Samasara and Nirvana, and so coming to Himself, as that which contains, and simultaneously is, All.

This return to our original nature extracts a high price, but only to the ghost in the plastic box. The ego, which has evolved from identification with the character on the screen, to that of the ego of the spirit united with its source, now has died. For the original awareness, this is release, yet it finds itself to be unchanged and knows it has never been any different. To friends and family, the symptoms of this final ego-death may, or may not, be visibly dramatic. The trauma of release is indicative of the size of the ego that dies, rather than of the nature of the underlying Reality. Any value we place on the size or spectacle of the resulting trauma of others may be due to our own need for distraction, and longing for continued sleep in our pride as sincere seekers. Facing our own coming headlessness is much more difficult than ruminating about the possible symptoms of the decapitation of others. Much of what may have happened in another's becoming may not have been made available for our personal viewing, and consequent judgment.

The worded description of this final state is something that has caused much consternation in seekers and teachers alike through the centuries. Perhaps the best that can be said about it, is what it is not. It is not an intellectual conclusion reached through deduction, no matter how astute. It is not a feeling-state, not matter how sublime. It is something we receive, though we give it to ourselves. We become It, rather than "get it," and then know we have never not been It.

In most schools, words such as "awareness," "witness," "absolute," and "void" are used to describe the causeless state, which we seek to become. An aware witness, void of any other qualities; an unbiased, empty Observer, having no cause, but being the cause of Itself, alone. A conditionless yet aware state that is itself un-conditioned and not witnessable by other than itself, there being nothing other than Itself. Any description one hears that adds a word or words after "I am," is not a description of the Self, but at most, a description of a symptom or view. Be very wary of those who claim unending Bliss and Peace, for any relative state calls forth its opposite, and is subject to change. You, and only you, will come to know what your final state is, and then, later, will struggle to find words to describe it.

Fisherman, Hiker, Driver: Who Am I?

Our aim is to become one, to have one permanent "I."
But in the beginning work means to become more and
more divided. You must realize how far you are from
being one, and only when you know all these fractions
of yourself can work begin on one or some principal
"I"s around which unity can be built. It would be
wrong understanding to unify all the things you find
in yourself now. The new "I" is something you do not
know at present; it grows from something you can
trust. At first, in separating false personality from you,
try to divide yourself into what you can call reliable and
what you find unreliable.
— P.D. Ouspensky

Somewhere in the past, I had the good fortune to learn to fish. It started out as curiosity and peer pressure, but mostly came from a desire to spend time in the wilderness. Since my better half at the time thought it inappropriate for a grown man to just hang out in the woods, a socially acceptable excuse was needed... fishing it was. It went from a part-time habit to a full-time obsession in short order, then vanished as quickly as the marriage. What remains is mostly an inability to come upon a body of water and not look at it with the eyes of a fisherman. As soon as I approach the bank, I notice an immediate change. I become the fisherman and slip into the habits of years stalking trout in countless streams and lakes.

For a few years, this habit was identified with: "I" was the fisherman. In recent times,

I've been able to simply sit back and watch this fisherman as he goes through his well-worn act. He's no longer me, for the "I" thought is no longer present in him. The fisherman is no longer in opposition to his environment, but is lost in it. He and the fishing are one, but who was "I"?

On a recent hike, I had the opportunity to see this character in action, this fisher person, and several more besides. I noticed a person who hikes. It was interesting to watch how he made decisions as to route finding, rationalizing the climbing of "just one more peak," how he resisted the inevitable coming of the end of the day; his confidence and skill. Like the fisherman, he was an old friend of sorts, having once been "me" too.

Later, when the day was drawing to a close, I noticed yet another "person" in the entourage: the fellow driving the car. This chap was by far the oldest of the group and the most set in his ways. He had been "me" at times for most my adult life, and behind the wheel during many episodes, some best forgotten, at least by the insurance industry. Now the strange thing about these persons, or little men, is that at some point I had said "I" to each of them. I had even said "I" to them in turns several times over the course of a day, interspersed with a whole zoo of others. Who are these characters, and what is this mysterious "I" that floats with ease from one person to another? And most importantly, why don't most of us notice this?

The truth of the matter is simple. The fisherman is the response to fishing, the hiker to hiking, the driver to driving, or the attempt at driving. They are the insentient response to a particular set of circumstances, just one side of the coin of an event. There is no "I" in them. The only thing that is present in all circumstances, and paradoxically free of them, is our simple awareness. We say "I" to the least and greatest of our response patterns, but never question the apparent absurdity. Instead of remaining fast "asleep," become the hunter of yourself. Stalk this "I" thought, see where it leads. To be identified with and trapped in the confines of circumstantial response patterns, one after another, without rest, is hell on earth and the cause of our needless suffering. To be free is to reside in that which does not change, yet is aware, and does nothing. Keep watch on this sense of "I," and see where it leads you.

The Path of Becoming: From Psychology to the Listening Attention

Can we get past the illusive psychology of the flight-or-fight syndrome and the resulting egocentric personality?

A discussion on how knowing yourself can lead to greater spiritual possibility. Through becoming objective to our own psychology or personality, we begin to take spiritual work personally, and thus Become.

I've come to see two dominant types of personality, especially in those involved in spiritual seeking or self-definition. These two types, though polar opposites in character, spring from the same cause: our mis-identification with the ego as the real "I" or Self. These two personalities are the twin modes of action formed from the ego's perceived threat of annihilation at the hands of the Not-self, the environment outside of the body. These types can be defined as the reaction patterns to each half of the fight-or-flight syndrome. What I define as the *sleepyhead* is the dreamer, the introvert, lost in their imaginations, the somnambulist type. The sleepyhead can be also defined by its opposite, the egocentric type or *knucklehead*. The sleepyhead flees, runs away and hides from the not-self while the knucklehead tries to control, project and manipulate the environment. Each is relatively unconscious of itself, and thus thinks its manner of dealing with the world is the right or correct way.

The egocentric or knucklehead likes to butt heads with and have control of everything. All has to be done outwardly through the ego to control and force conditions to being favorable to the ego. He stays in the right by learning to fight. The opposite reaction pattern is true of the somnambulistic or sleepyhead, who is lost in dreams and reverie. His reaction, instead of attacking the problem, is simply to ignore it through running away, hiding in dreams, and keeping the ego afloat by living in the imagination. This comes from the passive or flight reaction of the two different halves of the fight-or-flight syndrome.

Sleepyheads and their knucklehead opposites are simply two different unconscious response-patterns to the perceived threat to the individuality-sense by the world or not-self. We don't know we've fallen into identification with a mechanical pattern when we react as a sleepyhead. We may think we're even acting spiritually (being superior), in that *our* way is the *right* way. Through self-observation, we can come to see that it all stems from our past and whichever path, fight or flight, we happen to have fallen into.

Paradoxically, in trying to escape the threat of the world, we dive deeper into it by striving to become better and better sleepyheads and knuckleheads. That cannot cure us, since we are trying to solve the problem only on the level of the problem. Through psychology, analysis, and over-thinking, we plot to escape from our pattern, through our pattern, thus the pattern is never ending. The only cure, finally getting well, is in seeing ourselves as we really Are. We may become subtler in our self-delusion and think we're spiritual, but we still have not come to a true understanding. The cure begins when we get to the stage of raising mind, in learning how to stay in the moment: facing the present without self-identification with reaction, only.

We could not do this as children; we were helpless. But as adults, with the help of a spiritually oriented group, teachers, and friends, we have the chance to act in self-knowledge and find our way back to innocence and silence. This is often only brought about through trauma, which clears the pattern, at least temporarily, enabling us to glimpse the world from a clear perspective. This can lead into the listening attention, to being able to stay in the moment, without being identified with the animal reaction-pattern.

One of the dangers facing the sleepyhead is that when he hears a talk on effortlessness, mindfulness meditation, or the various schools that say there is nothing to do as we are not the doer, it sounds great. He jumps on this subject of effortlessness because it fits his ego pattern. He thinks he understands what they're talking about. It's only until after he comes to know himself, through hard practice leading to a realization, that he comes to understand that he did not know what effortlessness really was, that he had no idea of the Void, true detachment, or of not being the doer. He didn't have the true sense of it. All he had was a pattern of blocking things out through distraction, imagination, fear, pride, and laziness, *being in the reverie of the sleepyhead*. He mistakes being *hypnotized*, by dreams, reverie and moods, for doing nothing or no-mind. Habitual reverie is usually a sign of this mistake. Some people, being in reverie much of the time, may get quite defensive when it's called to their attention. A period of time in a group that practices confrontation might do wonders for pointing this out, if they can stand the tension.

Our society and home environment are our first teachers, forming the basic personality. Where did our basic reaction of either fight or flight come from? *It was a sane reaction to madness. We ran away from the moment because it was unacceptable. Thus, our innocence was lost, and we eventually became what we were running from.* The fearful or aggressive reaction to life and its tensions led to the destruction of innocence and removed the ability to stay in the present. Through cunning, we learned to escape the present, and eventually came to be asleep with our heads in the sand. All that we were left with is that very cunning, operating through fear or violence. Eventually, we became that which we despised.

A pivotal moment in my own loss of innocence came about at a young age one morning in my grandfather's backyard. I was playing with the gardener's son; we were fast becoming friends as the rapport deepened. I suggested that we should get together and spend the night at one of our houses and have dinner together. This was a relatively normal event at that age with other friends. He agreed, and we went to the gardener, his father, and proposed the idea. The look on his face when hearing of our idea is something I will never forget. Until that moment, I had not realized that he and his son were black, and that I was white. That he was the servant, and I, the grandson of his master. He told me in no uncertain terms that his son and I could never be friends. I then had a very clear moment of realization. I saw that the world of the gardener and my grandfather, and that of all adults, was insane. It was based on rules of behavior that were false and contrived, and yet somehow functional. I resolved then and there that I would never enter the adult state of mind. Decades later, I had the equally clear realization that this decision had somehow led me into the very state of mind I had sworn to avoid. I had become that which I despised: a fearful adult living in a false paradigm of isolation and ignorance.

This second realization and the circumstances that precipitated it, led me to the further realization that there was a way out of the action-reaction trap. I began to see that there was a third possibility, above and beyond that of child and adult. I had taken a small but sure step within. The subjective world of mindless action-reaction was replaced with a compassionate intelligence that had no interest in the ego games of the sleepyhead-knucklehead dichotomy.

We can't receive from the Higher or Inner Self if we are mechanical and asleep, emotionally and mentally, projecting an unreal "self" of unconscious psychology. To make contact with something Higher, we must find ourselves as observers rather than pattern-projectors. Raising mind, through focused attention in the present, leading to the listening attention, is a way to wake up for sleepyheads. Learning to listen, to have a passive but attentive reaction, can help knuckleheads to become objective. This listening attention, alertness without past or future worries, gives both types the possibility of receiving from the Inner Self. A rigid pattern-reaction solely based on the past is devoid of real intelligence, much less Being.

Being aware of who you really are in the moment, or the listening attention, is a wonderful paradox in that it's how we may stop the ceaseless mind chatter of the internal dialogue. Instead of stopping the mind chatter by force, by thinking other thoughts through an act of will, all we do is simply listen. You may find that there's something within that wishes to start conveying information, to tell you something that maybe you need to pay attention to. This quiet inner voice, our conscience, can only be heard when the mind is relatively quiet. Then, you can start seeing what your real problems are, why you're running from the present, and perhaps thus discover your deeper motivations, freeing your attention from the self-survival obsessions long enough to take a deeper look within. While you're in that state of listening, you can turn the attention inward and look within at what you're looking out of, and perhaps come to a startling discovery.

We're not going to make contact with the Inner Self, the source of wisdom, and find inner peace and stability, without setting up the right conditions. Now these right conditions are not as much an effort of trying to control something as much as a returning to what we might call innocence. We need to have a quiet mind, a stillness in the animal body. Overwhelming desires and obsessions must be faced and dealt with, cleared out of the picture. This doesn't mean we fight or control them, or runaway and ignore them, as much as become aware of them and see the difference between them and us. Then we can come to the point of focused attention in the moment, and possibly, the listening attention.

The daily remembering and clear admission of our internal angst is key to the eventual ability to face the moment. It gives us energy and incentive to separate from being identified with the psychological manifestations of personality in the drama of the sleepyhead-knucklehead, and how this misidentification traps our attention in the illusions of the mind. Once relaxed, we can jump straight into the still, aware silence: the listening attention. In other words, we go straight from personality right back up to what we really Are. We go from being a very complicated psychology, to being a very simple two-way seeing. We learn how to listen, to just look at the facts always in front of our vision, while simultaneously looking back at what we really Are. Psychological work is used only to show us that we don't have a quiet mind, no freedom of attention, and thus cannot tell the real from the false. Once we realize that having a quiet mind is something you simply find, it's always there just under the surface, you no longer have to think about it, put effort into it, build it up. It's a retreat from complicated error and projection back to the simple truth of ourselves as aware capacity, indescribable and real.

After we come to the psychological realization and self-admission that we're misidentified spiritually, that we have become our own enemy, even that which we despise, we can come back from psychological theory and find what we need to do; to take action rather than talk and analyze. We must say to ourselves: "now that I realize I do not know the truth, I also realize this way that I am does not work, that it has not brought me happiness or peace, power or fulfill-ment; *that there has to be some other way.*" Then we can begin to look within, and find what we really are through the listening attention. We see the value in being able to receive perceptions without the filter of our errant psychology. We no longer take our sense of "I" from the active personality-self, the psychological part we play as sleepyheads and knuckleheads. This sense of "I" has moved within, into our very *seeing*. We now take our lead, or our feeling of who we are, from farther within, rather than from a changing reaction-pattern to the world without. Now, "looking back at what we are looking out of" has a chance of becoming something more than clever words.

The point of all of this is not to make ourselves into more efficient persons, with better, more flexible personalities, though this may be the case. The point is to separate our inherent, basic awareness from the world of action or mind. Awareness and action are not mutually destructive. They can co-exist without interference. The problem is in the placement of our sense of "I." When the sense of "I" is lured into identification with the ever-changing picture show of action in the mind, the movement hypnotizes it and we are lost, separated from our Source in motionless aware silence. Through self-knowledge leading to pure observation, we can return to our true Home in simple awareness, no longer lost in the drama of movement in mind. Paradoxically, the play may continue, with the outer man remaining fixed in his pattern, whether a sleepyhead or not, but he will no longer be us.

The Hi-Jacking of Thought: The Paradox of Fear and Death

In spiritual work, we hear a lot about the so-called "false self." We may then decide, based on our newfound information, to distance ourselves from this "self," and look for something else we have heard of: the real "Self." This splitting of our "selves," sad to say, becomes just another trap of the mind to keep us lost in the realm of thought. After some honest self-observation, we may see that we have invented a problem so that we might continue unabated in our love affair with thought. Fearing a loss of continuity of thought, which we equate with death, we enter a new "spiritual" realm in which we can become lost for years, perhaps lifetimes. Let us take a look at this realm of thought and its various selves, and see why we worship it so, this paradox, this trap of mind and fear from which few escape.

Let's take a look at a man involved in ordinary life, and see how the circle of his mind works. He has a bad day at the office, where his boss berates him, causing a loss of self-esteem. He returns home and starts his daily meditation practice, intent on regaining some peace of mind after the trauma of the day. He meditates on things holy, on the words of wise men that tell him he is immortal, infinite, and serene, and that it's just that false self thing that is troubled and disturbed. His body calms down, and he finds a bit of energy, feels renewed, and the holy words of how he is Everything and One pump up his deflated ego until he feels he can face life once more. He is now reassured that the self he seeks through his spiritual ambition is the real one, and the false self the one that was deflated in daily life. He has convinced himself that one day he will make the real self permanent, and ditch the false one for good. But come later that night, his wife points out some fault of his, the kids are being kids, and he finds himself back in the dumps again. His resolve to be the better self is forgotten amid the onslaught of circumstance.

Now, if your goal is just to be a better person and get by as best you can, this all might not make sense, but if you've had the intuition that life, in thought alone, is a zero-sum game, let's take a look at the basis of our man's dilemma. He has, first off, become lost in thought, and secondly, believes that more thought will somehow release him. His ego has split itself into several objects. One is the judging, critical man who resolves to change, and dumps all problems on the heads of the others, including his false selves. These unlucky saps are the pairs of polar opposite selves, including the everyday man of action, whom he calls his "false self," and its twin illusion, the "real self" he aspires to, projected as innocent, perfect, and always just out of sight. The common ground of this menagerie is thought. All are patterns of thought. In any valid sentence structure we have a subject, an object, and a verb. It is the same in our man with one difference: he is lacking the verb, and changes from subject to object at the drop of a hat. The subject/object is the ego, or self, which splits and changes according to circumstance, and the missing verb is our basic seeing, the observer.

Our man's subject/object thought-patterns can be seen as two movies: one an inner drama of thought, memory and concepts, being basically reactions to the other movie: the outer world of the body. When the outer world, say the man's boss, delivers a negative shock, an affliction to the man's individuality sense, he is then forced to counter this in the inner drama with positive thoughts in order to maintain his ego. This is the real function of his so-called meditation; an attempt to get his ego back on its feet, and reaffirm his sense of existence. This cycle is self-perpetuating and circular; it never ends of its own accord. It is simply thought maintaining a belief in itself, through the fear of thought coming to an end. It is not spiritual, good, bad, or even real. It will only end when we no longer fear its end. Only when we can face the moment alone, without running headlong back into the realm of thought, do we have a chance of facing our self, much less actually going within.

This pattern of identification with thought is rationalization of fear and desire; it is not proper thinking. Thinking has been hi-jacked and is now used to keep the idea of our "self," itself a thought, alive. It is lying to one's self to keep the storyline intact. Thought is used to manufacture a "real self," which we aspire to, or believe in.

We then reject our present state, the "now" of seeing, the verb, in favor of an illusion that we desire, or an image we are running away from. Thus we are unreal, a thought. A thought endlessly forced to modify itself to avoid the present moment, for that would bring the facts into play and end the continuity of thought, which is seen as death. If we could just look, or observe, rather than thinking about what we think we see, we could "sit with" or accept what we see. This is to go within, rather than the seeking to bolster the "self" by thinking our way out of the moment. Thought is hi-jacked through fear, the fear of the end of thought. What a paradox, and what a trap, one in which the only true escape is through the very death of the fear of the end of thought. This dis-identification with our own mind will usually be considered only if it is forced upon us, by utter failure or trauma, baring intense true earnestness. We must uphold our pride in order to avoid facing the end of thought, our basic fear, and thus until our pride, our knowing, is so badly shaken that we can once again see clearly, we will not consider anything outside of our pride in our mind.

As U. G. Krishnamurti points out, we can never return to our natural state of enlightenment by the rearranging of our thoughts: psychological mutation. We must actually change what we *are*, our basic identity, and thus leave thought aside. We return to our true state, that of seeing rather than thinking. *But how?* The trap is almost foolproof. Any effort on our part is just more thinking, an unreal self trying to catch its tail, going ever faster until it flies up its own you know what. Some teachers tell us that earnestness is the key, that we must become so earnest in our search that we become a living vector towards truth. True, but definitely the exception to the rule. For most of us this lies farther down the road, and a little convincing might be in order first.

To gain this conviction, this earnestness, we can do two things. First, we take care of ourselves. We save our energy, however we can, and lead a simple, directed life. This gives our intuition a chance to mature, and our reason a chance to purify. Secondly, and here's the hard part: we learn to look, to listen, to observe. We learn to return our thinking to what it does best, which is running the practical matters of life, such as earning a living and fighting traffic. Then, free of plotting and planning our future victory over the universe and ourselves, we instead take up the arduous task of self-observation. Life will give us plenty of opportunities for this, if we are brave, and learn to sit in the silence within. We can't look directly within at first, we would only be indulging in fantasy and escape. But we can learn to look at our sense of "self," when life threatens this sense. Next time you feel a threat to your basic sense of existence, to the thought of who you are, instead of running away or countering it with another thought, *simply look at it.* Thus we retreat from thought, backing within, in an oblique manner. This also gives one a sense of direction, of where "within" really lies. When thoughts arise and the spin of thinking comes rushing back, don't go with it, but sit quietly and just look. Accept the pain of the ego in its fear of death, and look at its root. Look at the fear, the need to run away into distraction and thought. Stay focused, quiet and brave, and allow yourself to be in the moment. After a time, you will come to know this direction, the way within, and will come to look at your troubles as opportunities for further meditation. The sense of being the doer or subject will fade, the attention will be freed, and thought will be seen for the reaction it is. Motion and mind will no longer be your "self," and listening with attention will be valued more than plotting. This is true meditation, and the road Home.

Where Are You Headed?

Do you think you will automatically go to a spiritual place after death? Will you have the drive and capacity to determine your fate and direction when the body/mind dissolves? Do you know yourself that well? What will you have for guidance? Or will the unconscious desires and fears of today, which you may not be aware of or admit to, control your fate?

After our death, we may not find ourselves in Happy Heaven, as we might wish, but instead in a place formed by our true motivations, whether we were conscious of them or not. Instead of getting an eternity at The Warm-Fuzzies Fun Park, the more accurate scenario may be akin to when we fall asleep at night, letting go of our so-called conscious control and helplessly entering the world of dreams. This could be likened to the Tibetan concept of the bardo, with the experience of lucid dreaming (knowing we are dreaming while in a dream) thrown in to boot. In other words, if you can't wake up to Reality now, what makes you think you ever will? This dream world or bardo you may find yourself in would become the current dream or "reality" in which you again act out your previously formed nature. Whether any of this is fact or fiction isn't the point. What is being asked is, do you know and trust yourself well enough to face death and what it might bring?

There is a lot of talk of lucid dreaming nowadays, but I have yet to hear of any of it reaching a valid point in terms of true self-definition. Anything we learn or experience in a dream, lucid or not, must be validated in waking life. We might be advised to wake up first from this present dream of life before playing about with states of ego-identification in our dreams. Acting out our fantasies in dream land in a so-called lucid state is not a true awakening, but simply extending into the dream realm our identification with the personality. Even though much of the talk about lucid dreaming is astute and intellectual, providing much theory and heady adventure, rarely does it touch on the big questions of our personal life and death, and even rarer does it take on the question of "who" is dreaming.

Years ago I learned how to practice lucid dreaming, thinking I would become a hero shaman, weaving magic while discovering deep secrets in the freedom of the dream world, wide awake. When I actually found myself in the dream world, wide awake, the first thought that came to me was "I can do anything I want, I'm awake in a dream!" I must explain that at this time I still believed I was in control of my thinking, that I had thoughts. It was only much later that I came to realize they had me, that all thought is projected upon us. The next thought I identified with was, "Let's do all the things we can't do in regulated society, let the party begin!" I quickly created a fantasy sex partner and off we went, for a brief moment. The fun was rudely interrupted by the realization of how divided my consciousness had become. I was shocked that my true motivations, though unconscious, were not only carnal, but degraded. I was not the hero dream warrior I had imagined but a depraved animal. I thankfully fell back "asleep" in the ensuing turmoil of emotion. I dropped the experiments, for I realized I lacked the true self-knowledge and control that I had assumed I possessed. This was also accompanied by the intuition I was entering dangerous ground without adequate protection. This example may seem extreme, but it illustrates the point.

In the time that followed, I began instead a simple practice of dream interpretation, designed to help bring the unconscious world within up into the light of day. Thankfully, things were not really as bad in there as I had feared, but many unflattering facts and negative traits were uncovered and eventually faced in waking life. Much help was found in this endeavor, and I'm still grateful for being led back into truth from foolishness. Blindly following our animal nature and its promptings, whether in the dream world or out, only leads us through endless cycles of struggle and misery, desire and fear, with no true reckoning or resolution, forever and ever, amen. Real knowledge of the self is more valuable than any dream adventure, no matter whether we are "awake" as our daytime ego in the dream or not. Sooner or later we will tire of the fantasy, and perhaps become curious of "who" is experiencing these endless never-never lands.

True adventure is not in outward grandiose imaginings, whether in waking sleep or whatever, but rather in *a steady inward movement*, an uncovering of all that is hidden and false in ourselves. It is the greatest expedition we can make, for it leads to real peace and true awakening. This precipitous moment of turning our attention around and looking within is worth more than any bardo of lucid fantasies, for it can lead to real Self-knowledge, to Who we really are. As G.I Gurdjieff said, "Life is real only then, when I am."

True Direction

If we wish to find our Source, our True Self, then, as in looking for anything, we will need a direction. As Meister Eckhart admonishes, "if we wish to find God, we should look in the place we left him." We can only find that which is real if we look for what does not change and therefore is not projected from our own minds via memory. If we are possibly eternal, then we must have been before the body and before the brain, and even before our own mind. If God is eternal, and we are as him, then he was there before the mind, too. We left God by going into, and becoming identified with, the body/mind and its everchanging flux. To find God, or our Source, we must therefore go back, not further out into the wilderness of the mind, the matrix of images. These images are secondary to the mind that creates and projects them, so how can we give them greater meaning than the mind, and even to our observing of them? What is required is a reversal, a retreat, a *going within*. This will naturally lead us to look in an inner direction, away from images drawn from the memory, and even the image-creating mind itself.

The one constant is that we can be aware of all of the above. This ever present awareness, which is constant and indefinable, is the only unchanging fact. The images can be made to have value that changes according to memory, circumstance, or an agenda of the ego, and as such are on a lower level than that which is aware of them. The fact of this is seen through the process of going within, by retreating from the images themselves, the image-making process and projection, the memory, and even any concept of an individual "self." To put our faith in any image, whether of an idea, personage, or institution, is to go out and away from the source. To turn towards the source and leave the images behind, is to turn within and find what remains when nothing remains but that which is aware. This "still desert" is frightening, for it means the death of the ego, which cannot live without an image from which to draw its existence. As long as we turn away from our Source, lost in the finite flux of images, how can we come to know we are the Unknown? Look fearlessly within; a timeless field of awareness that is everywhere and nowhere awaits.

Back of Beyond

There is a place of Quiet
back beyond your hopes, fears, your dreams.
Don't listen any longer
      to those thieves.
           They lie,
as they keep you gazing stupidly at the patterns
bouncing about your fevered mind.

Listen instead for Silence,
quieter than a tiny bug crawling through dry
leaves somewhere
behind your fear.

Listen to your Self,
answering your own prayers back beyond
thought,
in the silence behind your head,
before your memory, after your death,
beyond your dreams and desires,
         and your anger at their coyness.

Be still, there's no need to hurry.
We will all meet again,
in the quiet peace before our names were born…
          back of beyond.

Movie Madness

The Cathars believed that their soul became trapped in the world, reincarnating over and over until they were once again free from identification with this dimension and could return home to pure Spirit. They saw how our attention becomes easily trapped in this dualistic universe. Snared by the temptations of the outer life, the mind creates an inner thought-based world to match, and by these very thoughts, reinforces the outer world of matter and the senses. Seeing how thoughts and matter became intertwined, creating a net nearly impossible to break, the Cathar Perfects labored to save themselves with great earnestness. A little serious introspection will show us that we too are trapped in a net of two worlds interwoven of mind and matter.

The first of these worlds, and the primary projection, is the physical world of matter and the senses. It is basically neutral, having no emotional or value-based characteristics in and of itself, and separate from us, being a view. This world includes our body, also. The second world, our personal inner drama, is entirely in our heads, and is reactive, less real, and layered upon the first world like icing on a cake. It too, is only a view. The only reality in either of these worlds is our attention, which, when it comes into contact with this dualistic mess, soon becomes trapped.

These two worlds, or movies, let's call them, are so intertwined that we come to see them as one. We are taught from birth to accept what we see in front of us as real, and soon learn to accept our inner reactions, or thoughts, as valid also. Most of these early thoughts are colored by the psychic atmosphere of our home environment, and are never questioned, being so close, and us so young. Soon enough, as the play of life unfolds, we have blended our thoughts and the scene before us into one big drama, which we call our life. This so-called life oscillates between heaven and hell, depending on how the two movies are interacting. Barring a catastrophic failure, trauma, or mounting misery, we never question any of this. Any attempt at escape usually consists of simply rearranging one of the two movies to better fit the other. Let's take another look at each of these dramas, and see if we can find any holes in this net; the trap of movie madness.

The first movie, the world "out there," is the universal projection we are all, as humans, subject to. It functions according to universal rules, and can be taken as good or bad, right or wrong. Hardly anyone sees it clearly, in and of itself. To illustrate this, simply pick an object and try to look at it without association. If you could see the world as it is, without benefit of the inner drama's projections, you would not know what the object was, nor care. As soon as "knowing," or memory, kicks in, you are looking at the inner movie as it layers itself over the neutral world of the senses. For most of us, many years of inner work are necessary before we can gaze upon the world without attachment. This can be a startling revelation, to look about at a world created new every moment, full of wonder and possibility. This listening attention can only be had in a quiet mind cleared of emotional baggage, a mind unconcerned with voices of judgment and fear, desire, and greed.

The other drama, the inner movie, is the world of thought, both personal and impersonal. It is reactive, associative, and entirely in the head of the individual, regardless of how it may or may not correspond to the heads of others. It is what separates and confines. Again, to get a look at this, pick any familiar object, and take a look. What you tell yourself you are seeing is your inner movie at work. If you see the object as separate, with associations in memory, no matter how valid, you are looking at your own head, not the object. As you go through your day, look at how everything you see is colored with memory, expectation, and judgment, trapping your attention into a dualistic dream world of your own creation. And it all happens automatically, as if by magic. And magic it is. We weave and spin the net that binds us into our own heads with every thought we identify with. How can we free our trapped attention, and perhaps turn it back in the direction of our Source, towards something non-associative and changeless, something Real?

The devil is said to be in the details, and this is where we can start. Simply look at your thoughts, your reactions, as they automatically fire every second of the day. There are many holes in the net, if we but look. By a constant passive attention, a listening, a looking without thinking, we can spot the many little clues that show us how we project the inner movie onto the outer, and how we can break the chain of relentless association. Once this listening attention is familiar, one can learn to turn it, to move it from movie to movie. We may eventually find it can be turned around and focused within, behind the inner movie to the formless realm beyond all experience. This freedom of movement of the attention doesn't happen by willing it, for that would be just another ego-character playing about in the inner movie. It simply happens, once we've paid the price.

If you're not lucky enough to have paid the price of losing your own head through the grace of trauma or disaster, then the freeing of your attention must be bought with austerity, conviction, and earnestness. The Cathar Perfects gave us a hint on how to get started freeing the attention through their lives of abstinence, discipline, and peace, which set them free from the cares and temptations of the worlds of matter and thought. This lifestyle develops the intuition and clears the head of desire and fear-based thinking. Then, by paying constant attention, coupled with intuition, one can see little tricks, gaps in the net, that build on the conviction that things are not as they seem. The inner presence of one who has already lost his head can also help. If felt, this presence may trigger a revelation, a conviction that there is something beyond the apparent. As for earnestness, this cannot be bought or faked, but again can be bolstered by intuition, clear reasoning, and the facing of the fact that life, as it is in appearance, is a zero-sum game.

The everyday world of paying the bills and getting by will not allow itself to be questioned; it will not help you of itself. If you have read this far, you must have seen enough holes in your own net to start questioning your worlds, inner and outer. If so, make a move. Find your true companions, the ones who too have had enough of the dream world of living alone, in the movie theater inside their heads. They're out there in the lobby, waiting for you, these soon to be headless souls. Help each other, clear a path through the tangle of thought and form. Find the exit, the door to daylight and freedom, and walk away from the movie madness of shadows and dreams. You may discover, once you are outside in the daylight, that you and your companions are One.

What Do You Love?

If a thing loves, it is infinite. — William Blake

Progress on the spiritual path can be thought of in terms of value, or love. What is most important to us is what we value the most, what we really love. The path of self-discovery can be seen in these terms. We observe ourselves, and discover what our true motivations are, leading us to see what we value. Another way to see this is by checking our fact status. What we actually do everyday tells us much about what we value, and perhaps shows us the gap between our personal storyline and our actions. If this fact checking and self-observation are carried far enough, we may begin to get a look at something called our "self" or personality, and begin to see its illusive nature. We may be forced to admit to its exalted status as our real true love, despite our ego's protestations to the contrary. Using this shock as further fuel for the search, we become a bit more honest in our future assessments. If self-inquiry is carried even further, through this process of elimination we may find something more real to love than this "self." Back beyond our mind's motion, something still and silent lies. If you find a love of truth, rather than fiction, it may take you there.

Finding this still-point depends largely on our state of satisfaction with our beloved "self." If the state becomes one of dissatisfaction, we have the incentive to look for something more stable. Hearing from others that have gone before that there is something somewhere "within," and that it is worth any effort to find it, also adds to our incentive. By looking at what we love, we can come to love the truth, and find there is something worthwhile inside us other than mind-motion and change. Let's take a look at how this path might turn out, and some of the pitfalls and signposts along the way from love of "self," to Love Itself.

We hear of this so-called still-point, called by such names as silence, stillness, the center, the Source, what we really are, etc., and wonder. If our intuition is not clouded by the dissipations of relentless pleasure seeking and the resultant fear, we may discover a longing, a nostalgia deep within that tells us we may have once known this silence, and still love it more than we might know. This longing is fed too, perhaps, by being tired of the jostling effects of life, its traumas and endless no-win scenario, leading only to death and dissolution.

So, we read the books and search the Internet, finding many who tell of the way back to this stillness. They vary from the intellectual work of Hubert Benoit, to the practical experiments of Douglas Harding. We find the paths back to this center also called by many names: "the inner movement," "self-remembering," a "double-pointed arrow of attention, one directed in, one out," "observing the observer," "looking back at what we are looking out of." Many speak of "silence," and even the many forms of silence. From this information alone, we may not come any closer to really knowing this still-point, but if we persist in looking, we may get lucky and discover much that it is not. We begin to see that it cannot be something of the mind, for we find the mind is motion. We may be fooled into thinking that the stillness is something we can manufacture, that it's found only in ashrams or monasteries, or that we can force it onto the relative world through controlling the environment. Or we may decide to create it within by controlling our mind, forcing it to think only what we have been told we should think, and discover that this too, is folly.

When the still-point is finally reached, even if only for a moment, it is unmistakable. If we have allowed ourselves to hone our intuition and clear our thinking, we will find that this silent place within is not just a concept, but very real. The movement necessary to turn our attention back away from the outer and inner movies of the mind and senses is found to be also something real, and not a thought or concept at all. We find too, that we forget, and are carried back into the mind at every instant. But if our love for the silence is true, it will turn us back into it again and again, provided our previous experience with the mind and its motion has been enough, or too much.

This is where what we value or really love comes in. If our meaning is taken from the changing scene of the relative world, we will keep our attention directed towards it. We will turn away from the silence within, and our longing will be for the excitement and changes of the mind. We may declare our love for the center, but our attention will long for the agony and ecstasy of the world of form. Boredom with silence too, means our value has not yet moved inward from the world to truth, but remains trapped by the colorful kaleidoscope of the mind, and the energy releases of the body.

This part of the journey is a journey within. We retreat from our former love for motion and change, and move inwards toward simplicity and truth. After the still-point has been found, and correctly valued, our attention is then turned round, and we begin a new phase, one of our new love being tested. While we continue to hold a part of our gaze on the still-point, it being what we really are, we also turn round and engage in the world of action. This is to test our love, to see if the trials and tribulations of the outer world can knock us off course, and change our point of reference. If we come back to the center, time and time again, during and despite every trial, we find we are becoming less of the world and more of the silence. In any situation in life, no matter how difficult or how often we forget, if we eventually return to the still-point as our anchor, we find we are becoming one with it. We become that which we love.

The Dividing Mind

Every last one of us thinks we are right.
— Richard Rose

Our mind has an amazing ability to split itself. The effect of this on the seeker of self-knowledge is to lead him about in endless circles of egos, never getting a true look at himself. "The world is divided into people who think they are right" also applies to the world inside our heads. The ego has to maintain this position of being right, or the center of the universe, in order to keep its position as the unquestioned "I." It accomplishes this by splitting into different roles. This is the Ego 1-Ego 2 game, in which the main ego, or Ego 1, creates a scapegoat, Ego 2, on which to place all negative aspects about itself. It cannot be wrong and maintain its absolute rule, so when the facts speak otherwise, Ego 2 becomes the culprit. The variations of this are legion. Thus, a ceaseless internal conflict is perpetuated and any attempt to go within is effectively blocked. And we wonder why the unexamined life is misery.

This process is started long before memory, when the parents use this same escape mechanism on their children. The parent keeps its attention away from its own negative aspects by using the child as Ego 2. The child is then taught the trick, growing up using this mind-splitting to remain "right" regardless of the facts of its own behavior or thoughts. The voice of the parent will remain in them, goading them to create their own endless versions of Ego 2 as facets of their personality, to be planted eventually in children of their own.

This process can be seen most clearly in extreme cases where either trauma or frustration reached such a level as to cause the mind to escape by creating another "person" complete with its own world. In cases of trauma so intense as to be completely unacceptable, the mind may create a new, safe personality and forget the former one, which was subject to the traumatic event. All conscious connection with the traumatic event is thus lost. In cases of frustration or extreme boredom, the mind may compensate by creating a grandiose paradigm in which to reside, where it lives in inner fantasy to escape the "average" existence of the fact state. The ego cannot tolerate "average." "Always remember you're unique, just like everyone else." In either case, the mind has succeeded in creating a refuge where it can remain "right." This is all simply a mechanism of nature to insure that the individuals of the species do not self-terminate prematurely. The sad part is our ignorance of it all, and our continuing identification with the mind's creations. We are not very good at observing ourselves, but most excellent at creating new "selves" and their worlds.

If we come to the point where no fantasy will do the trick, however grandiose or safe, and where we begin to see we are not "right" or "wrong" but simply ignorant, we may begin to yearn for something more than the ego can provide. The Inner Self is continually trying to draw our attention to how we fool ourselves, and relentlessly showing us how to get back in touch with the facts. This is an inner process to which we have a right and need, and with which we can reconnect. It lies beyond the ego-centric position, and comes about when we start to observe ourselves rather than create or visualize "selves" we then identify with, in either a positive or negative manner. The adage "know thyself" now has new meaning. It does not say "if you don't like what's happening, but wish to stay identified with the manifest, create a new 'you'." Learning to observe, or listen, takes courage and patience but leads to an amazing situation. You become everything when you are not anything. There are many techniques that can help us learn to listen. In the quiet of a mind at peace, the tools of dream interpretation, intense self-analysis, group confrontation, time alone in contemplation, and even life itself can teach the earnest seeker what he is not, and how to re-establish contact with the Inner Self. Listen with attentiveness; the Inner Self may be heard above and beyond the mind-splitting clamor and dis-ease of the ego and its creations.

The Mechanics of Dreaming

Disciple: But how shall I comprehend this Ungrund
(this naked Ground of the Soul, void of all Self)?

Master: If thou goest about to comprehend it, then
it will fly away from thee; but if thou dost surrender
thyself wholly up to it, then it will abide with thee, and
become the Life of thy Life, and be natural to thee."
— *Jacob Boehme*

As spiritual seekers, we should become at least as aware of how we are built inside, as we are of our anatomy. Our mind and its workings should be as familiar as the wiggling toes on our feet. Sadly, this is seldom the case. Let's take a look within our machine and see what's really happening in the inner realm of thought and feeling.

To start, let's perform a simple experiment. Ask yourself the question, "How do I feel?" Then, take a good look at what happens, inside. You may answer in different ways, in the positive or negative, and then perhaps wonder if you're right or wrong. This is all not going to help, no matter the answer, and is what most of us do, seekers or not. Instead, try looking a little deeper, and quicker, at what really happened. When the question is first asked, a strange thing occurs. The mind projects an image of what it currently believes "I" to be. It holds this image up in the attention, so that the feeling center can get a good look at it. This feeling or emotional center then has a reaction to this image of "I," of what you take yourself to be, at the current time and circumstance. Then another strange thing occurs. The mind that created the initial image modifies it according to the emotional signal it receives from the feeling center. (If you're feeling-oriented, the process could be reversed, with the feeling reaction noticed first, then the projected image.) This brings us to the question of where did the mind get the original image it projected? It was just the most current version of this created image, brought on by the endless and fully automatic cycle of thought causing feeling, causing more thoughts. From this, we can see the importance of discovering our own dominant moods, chief features, and states of mind, which all fuel and mold the above process of creating an "I" that we then identify with. We unquestioningly believe in this "I," till death do us part.

Now we have to back up a bit and get into this business of identification, and the observer. Most of us are predominately identified with either feeling or thinking, and our main sense of "I" is in one of these functions or the other. The weaker of these is usually negated, and the brunt of much abuse by the ego centered in the dominant function. The trick is to bring both of the functions into full consciousness, and to get behind them. To observe them rather than just identify. To unconsciously identify with the mechanical reactions going on in the mind is to stay asleep, believing in the dream we're unconsciously creating, which is based on the previous dream, ad infinitum. Direct contact with the inner self or higher power is impossible when this chain of mechanical reaction is running rampant. Not a good way to live, if you think about it.

Let's ask the question again, and see what happens. "How do I feel?" Be quick. You have to be awake and watching *before* the process gets moving. Can you see the image you project of who you think you are? Now, watch the feeling center have a reaction to this image. Then the resulting modification or acceptance is applied to this image of "I." If you try this in a very relaxed state, free from stress or worry, desire and fear, you may get lucky and see nothing. You may see nothing but an attention or awareness that looks within the quiet mind, sees nothing but silence, and then looks to the now silent feeling center, and sees nothing. No reaction, because there is no unquestioned belief causing the mind to project an image, which you then identify as "you." Now, wait until you are under stress or in a bad mood, or excited and feeling good about yourself, and ask the question again. The feeling center will be sending out a constant emotional signal to the mind, which will be obliging enough to create the appropriate image. Teamwork at its best, eh? Both of these reactions, the image-making apparatus and the feeling reaction, are mind. But where are *you* in all of this?

The impartial observer is not found by simply denying one half of the mind-team, and thus claiming the death, or victory, of one's ego because you have ceased to have emotions; or to think you have stopped thinking, and entered "no-mind." Such sophistry will soon enough be put to the test. The solution lies in the trap of identification, in the misplacement of the "I." Lead the attention farther and farther within, until you have fallen behind your self, behind the mind. In this back of beyond lies Nothing, Boehme's *Ungrund*, pure Silence. From then on the images and emotional reactions of the mind will be seen as simply as one sees those wiggling toes.

Fact & Fantasy

Zen is walk, don't wobble. — Richard Rose

Many of us go through life enamored of ourselves to the point of not really knowing where we are headed or why. We refuse to question our decisions in any meaningful way, and only after a severe shock or trauma will we ever admit we may not have been what we thought. One of the dominant features of many seekers of truth is a feeling of superiority, which tends to blind the student to his own true life pattern. In other words, we live in our heads, safely hidden from the facts of our real existence.

If we are lucky enough to be clobbered into wakefulness and the truth of our life through trauma or necessity (I have no interest in speaking to those who are convinced they are "ripe souls," needing only to wait in idleness for their coming release), we may find we have been blind to something Richard Rose called our "fact-status." For example, when I first entered university, I was so convinced of my own superiority that I never thought of cracking a book, never bothered to show up for class or take notice of the declining state of my health and mind. After flunking out my first semester, becoming hooked on drugs, and letting my teeth nearly rot, I was forced to re-evaluate my thinking. My fact-status could no longer be ignored, no matter how far I hid in inner fantasy.

The above pattern of self-conflict, while a bit extreme, illustrates the gap between our false image of ourselves and our fact-status. We are continually knocked off balance by this conflict, and instead of facing the truth about ourselves and acting accordingly, many of us simply re-group, re-invent, and continue to live *as if* the story in our heads were true. The ego refuses to see anything wrong about itself, thus denying that which asserts otherwise, fact or not. We continue to be lulled asleep. Falling off the log into the stream of unconsciousness, we are shocked awake and climb back up, only to succumb again to the ego's song of distraction and desire, wobble off balance, and again take the plunge. This continued stumbling between ego-fantasy and the shock of the facts eats up our time and energy. We can keep up the game when we are young, for a while, but sooner or later we tire, become isolated, defensive, and begin to crystal-lize. Any hope of finding something beyond the ego fades as the ego becomes all.

The above may sound hopeless. But balance can be obtained if we persevere, learning from our mistakes and those who have gone before us. Rose called the process of using what uses us "milk from thorns." By recognizing the ability of our own mind to delude itself, we can hopefully set up a system of checks and balances to insure that our idea of ourselves is, at least, somewhat related to the facts. This fact-checking can be brought about in many ways: through honest friends and family, co-workers and colleagues.

Another one is intuition, learning to listen to the small voice within. Most importantly, we can become more aware by learning to be honest in truly observing ourselves. This use of self-observation, which might be called the opposite of rationalization, is spoken of by every serious system of finding spiritual truth.

Now, there are some of us who say, "Why bother with observing myself, when the great teachers recommend inquiring directly within for the absolute?" To find the truth, or absolute, one needs to be a true vector of inquiry. The above examples of how we are not this true vector, or stable inquirer, show the myriad paths of fantasy in which we become entangled. Let us not presuppose ourselves to be something we are manifestly not. A quick check of our fact-status will show us how we are ready, willing, and able to be distracted from inner inquiry at the drop of a hat or wink of an eye. Learning to walk a straight line, upright and somewhat mentally sober, would be a good first step. Developing one-pointedness of mind first, we then turn this beam upon ourselves, now knowing the difference between fact and self-created fiction. We are beginning to have a sense of balance through wielding the sword of discernment.

By developing and using this power of discrimination on our own minds, we come to see how and where the ability to fool ourselves originates. We come to know our minds, and thus become objective or anterior to them. Through this process of separation from our former "self," and through a growing acceptance of our fact-status (things as they are), we find we have been practicing what may be called a practical form of self-inquiry combined with surrender, and have made real progress. When we look back on the delusions we so readily accepted and projected, we have to laugh at ourselves and our previous stumblings about. The value of this progress is not in that we have found reality but in that we have become better able to discern the real from the unreal, and thus have increased our odds of knowing reality if we ever do happen to bump into it. In the words of Richard Rose, "We must desire the Truth, and have a capacity for it else we could not receive it even if it came to us by accident." By learning to walk, not wobble, we keep from continually falling off the log of discernment before we get to the other shore. We become painfully aware of the games we insist on playing, and the fears we harbor, and realize we might not desire the truth about ourselves as much as we thought. We begin to see our true inner motivations, hereto unconscious, and thus have the beginning possibility of real self-inquiry through a stable mind, and real surrender through acceptance of truth.

The Gap of Time

The Gnostic's tale of the Demiurge, the arrogant ruler of the material world, gives us a clue as to the nature of our own prison, and how to escape it. Being himself created, a creature, the Demiurge's belief in his own infallibility is a lie in basis, and so must be continually bolstered. To accept the true nature of his existence would be unthinkable, for it would mean his demotion from absolute ruler to mere manager, a caretaker of sorts, rather than the True God. This he sees as death, and rightly so. Let us take a look at how we as ego, a reaction-pattern created from thought, make the same mistake, and how we can become free of this prison of projection and delusion.

When we become identified, we do not become identified with the world or the body. We actually fall asleep to the world or body, and become identified with the mind; meaning *we are identified with thought*. We may believe we are seeing things as they are, for we have never bothered to take a look at *how* we see, or *what* we are really seeing. The self-reflecting consciousness sees just that: a projected reflection of its own consciousness. This inner mind-world is a superimposed projection, built of thought that was formed throughout the person's life and the process of which he is completely unaware. We do not see this projecting process, for it is instantaneous and automatic. We only see the end result; a world made of thought, removed from the eternal Now through a gap of time.

This split-second from when we receive a percept and then react to it with thought, is this gap of time. This gap, though it be only a split-second, is a chasm wide enough to separate us from our very Self or Source. It is also wide enough to allow us to live in a world of reaction; a world of judging, thinking, and assumption. This dualistic realm is never stable, ever changing, and ruled by a tyrant whose very existence is after-the-fact. This tyrant is called ego, and is the very thing we have come to be. Our very sense of self has become identified with a reaction-pattern, removed from the present through time. This sad state of affairs is not only unreal, but patently dangerous. All of the world's ills spring from this illusion.

This illusion can also be called mind, or the inner drama. We live in this self-created drama, and must continually re-create it to keep our false sense of self somehow stable in an unstable world. Now, in our struggle for self-survival, our first reaction to hearing this is to dig in, to insist more than ever that we are in charge by deciding to take immediate action and remedy the situation with our new knowledge. We may decide to root out this egoic ruler who has deluded us for so long, and never again make the same mistake. Or, if our pattern is based in fear, we may decide to run farther into distraction and thought, hoping to be safe in sleep with the covers pulled tightly over our heads. Both of these reactions would be laughable if they weren't so common. Through our very effort to free ourselves, we trap ourselves even more. Through the arrogance of "deciding," the Demiurge has simply affirmed its self-declared infallibility. We have made the same old mistake, again. As the reaction-pattern, we have only reacted. Nothing has changed; the dream goes on.

How then, can we escape this prison of thought and time? Our very effort to escape binds us more tightly, and even the world of distraction and sleep provides no rest, being subject to drastic change through ever-reacting thought. The answer lies not in affirming our ignorance through thinking we now know what to do, but in our admission of the problem itself. Through the simple admitting that *we do not know*, we begin the homeward journey to freedom. We start with this surrender; then our attention has the possibility of freeing itself from the drama of the mind in time.

This surrender is a not a passive giving in to our identification with the world or thought, but an acceptance of the facts. We realize that we do not know ourselves. We do not know how we see, much less what, and are thus freed to start looking. This admission frees our attention from the hypnotic trap of conceptual thought, and stabilizes it in silence. To find the possibility of moving this attention within to find out who we really are, as the True Self, means that we must free this wandering attention from identification with thought, and allow its gaze to be turned back within, across the chasm of time and projection.

When we can actually view the world without association, meaning we are finally capable of admitting we know not what we see, we have found a valuable clue. We have now become an observer, capable of turning our gaze within. No longer lost in time and the projection of the associative mental world, there is now the capacity to move within. We have this new freedom because we are no longer locked in the after-the-fact reaction-dimension of thought. This is how honest self-observation gives us *possibility to become*, to become a real Observer. In the world of thought, there is none. We step out of our own way, and are freed from our personal demiurge as we allow the True Consciousness to come forth.

Containing Tension

We are cowards, and what we witness about us is a dynasty of fear in a playhouse of desires.
— *Richard Rose*

Most of us go through life with no clear awareness of our limited time and energy, but instead continue to plan and plot our way along as if nothing will ever really change. We live to have fun, known as the pursuit of happiness, making our forays into the world of pleasure from a base of imagined security. Driven by the fear that our security is tenuous at best, we rush to have even more fun, before the circle of our dissipation and paranoia collapses in on itself. We never question our motivations or bother to define what we mean by happiness, perhaps because of an inner intuition that that would take the fun out of it. Let's take a look at what this pursuit really is, and how it can be turned from a struggle downhill into frustration and bitterness into a change of being.

This pursuit of happiness can best be defined as the pursuit of a fading memory, a memory of a time when some outside agent gave us a thrill of such magnitude we can't forget it, or else it relieved our anxiety so well as to leave us in a state of unusual peace. Being creatures of habit, we try repeating the same sequence of events that gave us the previous result. This cycle is sooner or later found to be one of ever-decreasing returns. We find the thrill or release lessen, while the inducing agent is needed in ever greater quantity. We never question the process itself. We never wonder why we even need an outside agent in order to feel happy, at peace, or complete. Only when the agent turns on us, and becomes the deliverer of pain and misery instead, do we stop. Even then, we still seldom question the process, but think we can beat the system by getting a new, improved agent and becoming cleverer in its application.

As incredible as it sounds, an unhappy man does not realize that happiness is better than unhappiness. Knowing only his own concealed anguish, he worships it, which is the same as self-worship. — Vernon Howard

This unconscious trap of worshipping our own weakness keeps us from becoming strong. We fail to realize that the tensions we feel, as anxieties or promptings, are the very things that will free us from all need, if we stand up to them. By giving in to every prod and poke that comes into our consciousness, we give away our time and energy to nothing, and keep nothing with which to build our mental strength and intuition. Through resisting these daily irritations and promptings, we save our vitality and time, which can then be put to use on the spiritual path. We also become something, something that has a greater capacity. We can think clearer, have more time for study, and come to have a resistance to the inner noise, which used to send us running for distraction or numbness. We will have increased our capacity for storing tension dramatically, much like putting our money in a bank that pays high interest, to be used for something of true value when the time presents itself, rather than spending every dime in our pocket, and relegating ourselves to living paycheck to paycheck. Eventually, we will also have gained enough inner quiet to possibly hear something from within, giving our intuition a chance to be heard.

Be very careful that you do not unconsciously assume that nervous tension is power. This is vital. Watch yourself the next time you work toward some goal. Look very closely to discover tense feelings and nervous thoughts whirling around inside. Do not let them deceive you into assuming that they are creative forces; they are not. They are thieves of genuine powers. As always, your awareness of their thievery is your first fine step toward casting them out.
— Vernon Howard

The energy we feel as excitement or thrills, is not the energy we are after. This is just the frenzy of a nervous mind, of thoughts and needs wanting to take advantage of us in exchange for a brief moment of peace when our stolen energy is gone. True strength and peace is in an increased capacity for tension. By increasing this capacity, we increase our resistance to the effects of life. We become calmer in the face of stress, and can think clearer under pressure. By virtue of our increased intuition, we may even begin to see through many of the traps we formerly succumbed to. Our patience will increase, and we will not panic and run when unflattering truths about ourselves come into the light of day. We will be able to sit and meditate for the lengths of time necessary to gain insight into these truths about ourselves, no longer giving into distraction, fear, or pride.

Through this reversal of the trap of dissipation into the discipline of containment, we gain a chance at freedom, and have become something more than a utility of forces unseen. We now have the possibility of using our limited time and energy in real ways in the pursuit of self-discovery. Our imaginary life of having our cake and getting to eat it, too, becomes instead a life with a true direction, towards truth and self-knowledge leading to real happiness. The Kingdom of Heaven is truly within, and we will not find it by taking our pleasure and meaning from without, from the world and its ceaseless change and pain.

The next time you feel an inner prod, an urge, an itch from below that you know can only be scratched at the price of your peace of mind, do not think that relief is in doing what it wants. Try resisting, turn away. We graduate from crawling by gaining enough strength to stand up and walk. Walking upright depends on having enough capacity for tension to resist falling down. Be patient, and learn to walk without wobbling. The view is better and you can cover greater ground. By this resistance, become something greater than the world, and take your meaning and definition from the silent strength you then find within.

Something for Nothing

We are what we do, not what we think we do.
The fact that you don't act means you don't have
conviction. — Richard Rose

I've found as I get older that some of the seekers I meet are getting long in the tooth, too, and suffer from a lack of conviction (inability to act) brought on by a combination of age and success in life. They have time and money relative to their youth, but are reluctant to use them towards their spiritual path. Perhaps this is not done consciously, but could be that a life-time of work and struggle, not only in the outer world but also in the realm of personality, vanity, and ego along with the effects of aging, have left them almost unable to act any other way. The strange thing about them is their "conviction" of commitment to the spiritual path, and the simultaneous lack of ability to act in that direction.

The following is a list of characteristics peculiar to this type of fellow and some questions for him in the hope he will see, and resolve, his paradox:

- You have heard that all is One and there's nothing to be done, and have used this to cleverly rationalize your inability to act towards spiritual work.

- You have heard that one must work on oneself even while going about daily activities, but have used this too as a rationalization to avoid actual involvement in spiritual work, especially with others.

- You find the view pleasing from resting high on the shoulders of those seekers who have gone before. Why do you refuse to carry someone yourself, to continue the chain? Your spiritual work consists mainly of reading and ruminating, along with some so-called self-observation while going about your business. Seldom does it involve actual work, even less work with others, and never work for the Work.

- Your comfort zone has been made secure by years of effort. Do you think you will make the trip within to the Truth by this continued comfort, both mental/emotional and physical?

- Any suggestion of change is met with cleverness, for you have become averse to anything that might rock the ego from its throne.

- This vanity of being always right even extends to your ideas about the ego itself, as evidenced in your insistence that you will "destroy the ego," thus entering further into dichotomy. Most of this occurs because of a deep-seated vanity that you are special, and thus have no need to involve yourself with the struggles of the less fortunate.

- When facing confrontation about your lack of action, you put on a polite yet knowing smile. Your sense of superiority carries over into spiritual work, and is defended by very subtle yet effective masks.

- You gravitate towards those that flatter your vanity, and if the going gets tough, you get gone. This vanity is your biggest block, and keeps you from your inner self, though you think just the opposite.

- When your superior attitude is pointed out, it is rationalized by declaring that underneath you still suffer from a feeling of inferiority. While this may be true, it is seldom worked on, and never resolved.

- If a meeting or retreat is attended, it's usually only once, for if there is no immediate profit from it, you feel there is no reason to go again.

- The idea of work being profitable only after years of constant effort has somehow slipped your mind. Possibly because your vanity says you have "been there, done that," now it's time to relax and reap the rewards.

- You have found in business how to work smarter rather than harder and this gives you an edge over the competition, but what is it you actually do with this new found time?

- You expect teachers and fellow students to cater to your schedule and seem to have no sense of how much actual work and effort they have sent your way.

Do you have an understanding that they are actually working, in actions as well as words, to get you to do the same?

Do you think you could reverse the habit of feeling you deserve something for nothing, and start paying, with your actions, for what you take from teachers and fellow seekers?

Something for nothing is a valid method of work, but only if it involves between-ness. You trade your "something," the vanity of the ego and its suffering, for the inner self, which knows its own nothing-ness.

A Formula for Self-Discovery

I'm often asked how a seeker can increase their progress along the path. Sometimes the person may feel stuck, or simply wants to know the most expedient way to increase their vector. Looking back over my own life, I've found that one factor stands out. When I became a conduit for realization, passing it along to others, things took off. It's as if we agree to become a link in a chain, and pass on down the line that which was handed to us from above. This is not only a theory, but something we can, and must, actively do in our day-to-day lives. One may argue that if all is one, then this is just another illusion, but the rationalizations of the ego come easy and keep us stuck in our own mud, while active work may put tension on us in a way the ego can't handle.

I can best relate how this works along the lines of my hobby with photography. I've spent a lot of my time in the great outdoors, and for years refused to share this experience with others due to a certain ego. I felt that if I took pictures of my trips, it would somehow cheapen the experience, take something away from the purity of the pristine settings. Somehow this changed, thank goodness, and I became willing and inspired to do the work to bring a bit of what I was seeing back with me to share with others. I broke down and bought a digital camera, and the magic began. Some inner part of me that had been denied came back to life, and with it a better relationship to everything involved. The entire experience of hiking was somehow changed for the better.

At about this same time, I also bought my first computer and entered the world of email and the Internet. I was able to stay in touch with fellow seekers from around the country, and to share my experiences in the search for definition, as with the photography. Somehow this changed the belief that spiritual work was a solitary affair only, and opened doors of opportunity I had never dreamed of. I started a web site, and became involved with an online confrontation group. I began to move within; the connection was made.

William Samuel talks about much the same thing. He describes getting answers from within as Glimpses, and stresses the importance of sharing these. It's a double-sided coin, much like the chicken and the egg dilemma, in that we must get answers in order to share them, in order to get answers. But the process is not that complicated, if we just make a move. We become a conduit, a transmitter of realization, and the more we give, the more we get.

One trap worth mentioning here is that of keeping this all in one's head. We may think that by getting a few answers in the beginning of our search, we are on the path and need not put out more effort. Being comfortable in our life, we may not wish to rock the boat of our habits, and thus keep whatever intuitions we receive to ourselves, thus miring our spirit in a dream world. Our intuitions bear fruit when they are put into action and tested in life, and when found sound, passed along to our fellows.

All of the above is what might be called a law of manifestation, an equation as Samuel calls it, and it will work for whatever desire applies it, spiritual or otherwise. If one wants money, success, or security, this formula will work as well. This leads to a dilemma for some of us, in that we may not consciously know what we really want until we test ourselves by putting the formula into practice. This can be a paradox. If we believe we want enlightenment, and put it to the test through actions in our day-to-day life, we may find that what we really want is freedom from fear or a desire for power. While we have temporarily fooled ourselves, we have at least come to know ourselves better, and have thus made a move along the path of self-discovery. We may eventually uncover an intense longing for home, for something stable and real, which was only allowed to manifest as the mundane patterns of fear and worldly desire. This was long buried, and is what will provide the necessary pull to carry us farther within. To get real answers, we must come to have real and pressing questions.

One thing is for certain, if we do not make a move, a commitment to action, we will not leave the head-in-the-sand false safety of our dreams. A man asleep in his bed in a burning house may dream of oneness and ease as well as anxiety and need. *On the other hand, waking up may take effort, be difficult and even unpleasant, but is most necessary, too.*

Identification

The view is not the viewer. — *Richard Rose*

In the search for our true identity, no problem is more pronounced than that of confusing what we see and what sees it. We become so hypnotized by the endless parade of images we come to feel at one with them all. We lend meaning and value to what we see, until we believe we have become what we see. The mass of experiences we give meaning to are the pattern we come to call our "selves," and any new experience that happens along is judged solely by how it flatters or threatens this pattern. We have come so far afield from anything even close to what we really are, it's no wonder the journey home is difficult, and so paradoxical.

We are forever looking out of ourselves, for ourselves, and relying on what's not us, to tell us what is.

We find when trying to examine ourselves directly, we can't help but put associative images up on the inner screen of our mind. Let's try a little trick. Look at an object in front of you, preferably something still and relatively common. Just look at it. No judging, projecting, thinking, relating, associating, feeling, remembering; just look. If you can do this for even an instant, things may become clearer, calm, and still. This is the absence of the projecting mind. What's left? Nothing much. Only you, the eternal observer of mind and matter, the infinite witness of feeling and believing. Behind the precious intellect, beyond the hallowed hall of feelings, lies the listener. This unlimited clear space has room for all, and need for none.

Tricks

As individual points of awareness, our chief feature is one of identifying. We become whatever we stare at long enough, and we have been looking at the body/mind since birth. This hypnosis is so strong, most of us cannot escape it without help. The ego, being the clever, self-righteous fool that it is, will not let us accept this help, so we have to be tricked. Fortunately, the Powers That Be invented some very useful tricks to help us out. All tricks are for destroying the ego-centric fantasy that we actually exist, as the body/mind or anything else for that matter, and for freeing us from believing that there is such a thing as an individual "self." They serve to back the awareness out of the individual mind/memory and into the state of universal awareness, away from self into silent witness. Thus, a retreat or dis-identification from the mind and its projections is caused, hopefully leading to the realization of one's true self: the observer. Here's a few tricks to get you going but remember… they won't work if you actually believe any of this.

•   Trick of going against negative emotions: This helps lead us away from the extreme defensiveness of the ego-centric position. We believe we're doing good and being virtuous by not being negative, but are actually just moving away from manically defending the false or particular, i.e., the "self." This brings about an inner movement towards a more universal view where one thing, or self, is not set up against another. This trick is also known as "helping others," practicing virtues, etc.

• Trick of "know thyself": The point of this trick is to cause dis-identification with the individual memory pattern by becoming familiar with it: what we see is not us. Getting to know the robot leads, hopefully, to realizing it's not you. The information gained by knowing one's self isn't the point, it's the inner movement or retreat that counts. So, don't worry if you discover you're not the person you thought.

• Trick of effortless meditation: We simply watch our thoughts without being attached or affected. Again, we're led within, as this trick serves to unattach us from our personal reactive mind and places us in the universal rather than the particular. This trick has the added benefit of being quite peaceful.

• Trick of self-remembering, "Who Am I," meaningless Zen koans, etc.: These tricks are quite simple, and therefore very effective. The ego loves complexity and distraction, so the act of focusing the attention on an unanswerable, meaningless koan knocks the ego off its feet, for a bit. Eventually, we may become less afraid of the silent unknown. The movement back and forth between the formal (mind chatter) and informal (silent awareness following the shock of perplexity) might bring about a triangulation: the body/mind and accompanying "self" or looker may be seen for what they are.

• Trick of self-inquiry: Great trick for the astute, since they think they'll have it figured out in no time. Eventually, they might come to find they're not as clever as they thought. It can lead the inquirer to accidentally going within, thus being effective. At its best, it will cause a surrender, or ego-death, when the mind comes to a dead end, thus teaming up with the trick below.

• Trick of surrender: A most powerful trick in that we are led to believe we are doing something pious, and instead end up getting a good look at our pride. The trick is that we've never been in charge anyway, meaning we do nothing and never have. Surrender as an act of the prideful, pious ego usually fails miserably. This can eventually lead us to inquire as to what we did wrong, thus leading us back to the trick above. If both inquiry and surrender are practiced, we might trick ourselves right into a massive ego-death, so be careful... don't get tricked.

Other Titles from TAT Foundation Press

The Perennial Way: New English Versions of Yoga Sutras, Dhammapada, Heart Sutra, Ashtavakra Gita, Faith Mind Sutra, and Tao Te Ching, by Bart Marshall

Beyond Mind, Beyond Death, selections from the TAT Forum magazine

The Celibate Seeker, by Shawn Nevins

Solid Ground of Being, by Art Ticknor

For more information on the TAT Foundation, visit www.tatfoundation.org.

CPSIA information can be obtained
at www.ICGtesting.com
Printed in the USA
BVOW10s1241080617
486274BV00001B/13/P